GOOD ✦ OLD ✦ DAYS

Live It Again™

1942

THE SATURDAY EVENING

POST

W. W. Calvert

© 1942 SEPS

Dear Friends,

Nothing epitomized the social and political climate of 1942 in the United States of America better than one of the first big events of the year: the annual Rose Bowl game on January 1.

Less than one month earlier, the blood of American patriots had been spilled on Hawaiian shores at Pearl Harbor during the brutal surprise attack by Japanese bombers. War with Japan was declared almost immediately following that "date which will live in infamy." Many feared the next target for a Japanese attack might be the West Coast, and large public gatherings there were cancelled—including "the granddaddy of them all," the Rose Bowl game in Pasadena, Calif.

But the American spirit refused to be dominated. Rose Bowl invitee Duke University offered to host the football game in Durham, N.C., and Pacific

There was no doubt that our lives had been changed inalterably.

Coast Conference champion Oregon State, a 14-point underdog, accepted the challenge and the change of venue. So, less than four weeks after the bombing of Pearl Harbor, the Rose Bowl was played at Duke.

The rest of 1942 played out the same in American culture. There was no doubt that our lives had been changed inalterably, but we would carry on with determination, dignity, and yes, discretion.

This special yearbook will take you through those cherished days of challenges as America picked up the gauntlet and forged the foundation of ultimate victory. Through it all we might have had to make adjustments—like moving the traditional setting of a football game—but we would persevere.

And, you might ask, what was the outcome of that 1942 Rose Bowl played under the veil of newly declared war? Why, the underdog Beavers of Oregon State won 20-16, of course.

Contents

REPRINTED WITH PERMISSION FROM AGFA-ANSCO

LIBRARY OF CONGRESS, PRINTS & PHOTOGRAPHS DIVISION, FSA-OWI COLLECTION, [LC-DIG-FSAC-1A35351 DLC]

LIBRARY OF CONGRESS, PRINTS & PHOTOGRAPHS DIVISION, FSA-OWI COLLECTION, [LC-DIG-FSAC-1A34882 DLC]

NATIONAL ARCHIVE AND RECORDS ADMINISTRATION

In this *The Saturday Evening Post* cover, the apparent uncertainty in the eyes of this child is calmed by snuggling with a trusting friend.

Everyday Life

New twist in family life

Following the attack on Pearl Harbor, young men began enlisting in the military. In some cases, they were young fathers, leaving a void behind in a society where family life was still solid and engaged.

Despite the many enlistments which often created an empty space in the family structure where a husband, father or son had been, a strong sense of family still predominated the American home life. The traditional family, while altered by the effects of the war, still gathered for a meal around the table, still encouraged its children in their pursuits and still focused on togetherness in a time of change."

FAMOUS BIRTHDAYS

Charlie Rose, Jan. 5 Television journalist

Stephen Hawking, Jan. 8 Physicist in cosmology

Clarence Clemons, Jan. 11 "The Big Man," saxophonist for Bruce Springsteen's E Band

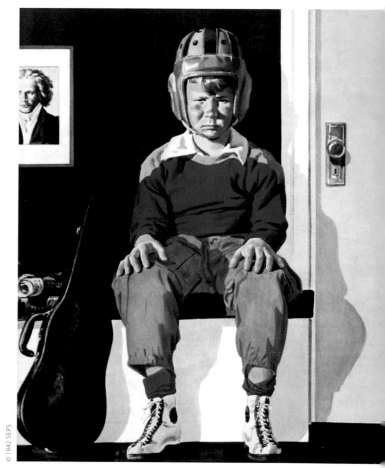

After-school activities, whether they were looked forward to or not, continued to be a part of daily life.

"So this is the supper I would have spoiled if I had bought a soda at four-thirty."

The Home Front

War's emotion shapes lives

American life in 1942 was shaped by the pain of "empty chairs" and the desire to strive for a sense of normalcy.

The difficult realization of loved ones in harm's way cast a sense of uncertainty into a world seeking the comfort of post-Depression prosperity.

The joys and tears surrounding the coming and going of loved ones added to the challenges on the home front, but despite those challenges, young love endured.

These difficult times brought a deep appreciation for the sacrifices of our ancestors and a fervent desire for peace and safety in our land.

"Black-out for a dime, sir?"

Tears of sadness often filled the eyes of those left behind in fear and concern over the lives of loved ones thousands of miles away.

The Home Front
Young love

It's not only men's stomachs that prove to be gateways to the heart. Sharing a bite of a hot dog during a quick break in the action proved to soften the hearts of both this Navy pilot and his friend.

Despite the fears tha came with having beau in harm's way i the war, this woma manages to smile, an make her officer smil in return, during moment together o the home fron

al Moor

The Metro Daily News
FINAL EDITION

MARRIAGE RATES
INCREASE DRAMATICALLY
Many tie the knot before the groom heads off to serve in the military.

It didn't take this sailor long to change his focus when his eyes were captured by those of his partner during a Saturday night dance at the club.

"Hey, Sis, your ship's in!"

Some things never change, including instant chemistry at the sight of an attractive girl. Even in the backdrop of war, the heart returns home for a brief rendezvous.

The Home Front

The battles were not only overseas

All wasn't always fair in love and war, especially when a discovery at the mailbox showed that a certain soldier was writing to two girls at the same time.

THE SATURDAY EVENING
POST

FAMOUS BIRTHDAYS
Carole King, Feb. 9
Singer and Grammy Award winner
Michael Bloomberg, Feb. 14
New York City Mayor
Joe Lieberman, Feb. 24
United States Senator from Connecticut

The Metro Daily News

FINAL EDITION

CHARLESTON, WEST VIRGINIA

FEBRUARY 2, 1942

PRESIDENT ROOSEVELT INSTITUTES YEAR-ROUND DAYLIGHT SAVINGS TIME

It will stay in effect until 1945.

After long months at sea, this sailor is easily tempted by a whiff of perfume and the charms of a lovely lady.

The Metro Daily News

FINAL EDITION

CHARLESTON, WEST VIRGINIA

FEBRUARY 10, 1942

AUTO PLANTS TO PRODUCE TANKS, AIRCRAFT, JEEPS

Last Ford car to be built until 1945 drives off assembly line.

"Very good, Mr. Murphy, but we will probably want you for noncombatant work."

The Home Front
Patriotism abounds

The American flag was the pride of the land, especially when proudly displayed by children marching with poise, honoring our troops at community events.

© 1942 SEPS

"All of a sudden they just popped out on me."

With Europe and the Pacific in turmoil, the Statue of Liberty, already an icon of American patriotism, became an even more significant symbol of strength and national values.

THE SATURDAY EVENING POST

The Metro Daily News

CHARLESTON, WEST VIRGINIA

FINAL EDITION

FEBRUARY 15, 1942

FIRST NEW YORK TIMES CROSSWORD PUZZLE APPEARS

Many who volunteered for service were often attracted by action-filled pictures of various military personnel serving in different parts of the world.

The Home Front

Rallying the troops

When the country was attacked, America's brave young men lined up to enlist, eager to avenge the assault on Pearl Harbor.

Recruiting posters touted all branches of the service as well as specialized skills that could be acquired in certain branches.

Interestingly, not all posters encouraged immediate sign up. Some, like the Navy poster below, encouraged those in college to stay there and participate in officer training along with their education.

A dedicated patriotic allegiance to the flag was all it took to attract many college students into volunteering for officer training.

High-tech occupations of the time, such as communications fields, often appealed to young recruits with the promise of lucrative job opportunities following deployment.

The appeal of Uncle Sam was so inspiring to wartime president Franklin Delano Roosevelt that he promoted it as a call to service in World War II.

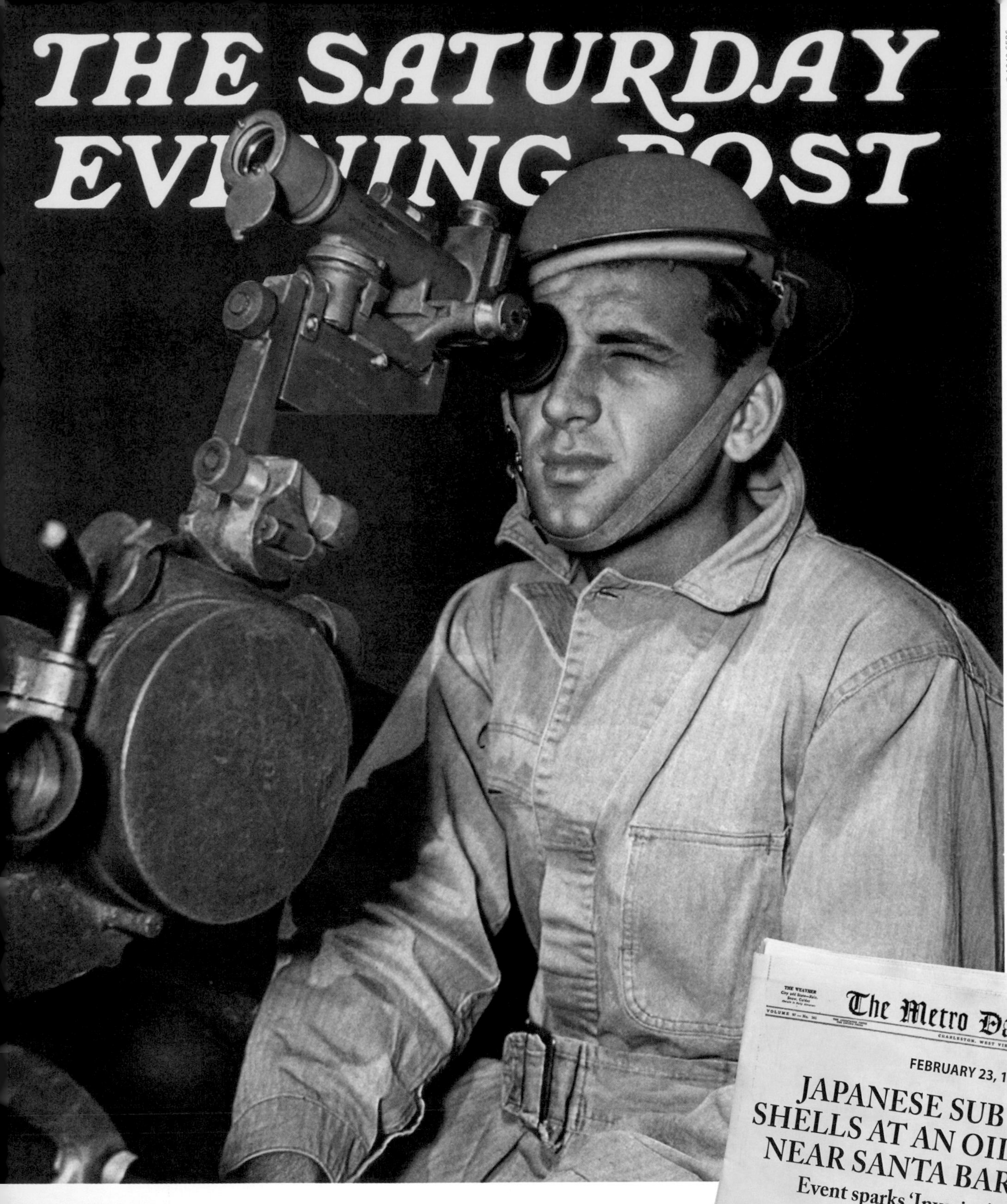

THE SATURDAY EVENING POST

American soldiers set their sights on images they had never seen before on home soil, such as enemy submarines and ships.

THE WEATHER

The Metro Daily News

CHARLESTON, WEST VIRGINIA

FINAL EDITION

FIVE CENTS

FEBRUARY 23, 1942

JAPANESE SUB FIRES 17 SHELLS AT AN OIL REFINERY NEAR SANTA BARBARA, CA

Event sparks 'Invasion' fears for U.S.

Men Go to War

Aircraft training

Hearts of mothers and fathers were broken in 1942 as their sons hastened off to war following the Japanese invasion of Pearl Harbor. Many families sent several sons at one time, often to both the South Pacific and Europe.

Emotions rose and sank at the war's escalation as sons enlisted and began training for combat. Training, depending on which branch of the military it was for, could include learning skills such as piloting, artillery use and tank operation.

An aviation cadet inspects his aircraft before taking to the skies from the Naval Air Base in Corpus Christi, Texas.

Pilots, like Lieutenant Mike Hunter shown here at the Douglas Aircraft Company, looked pensively into unknown futures.

Men Go to War
Mission briefings

Marine lieutenants stop to review exercises as they study to become glider pilots at Page Field in Parris Island, South Carolina.

Discussing plans before taking to the skies at night was especially tedious when many ground lights were out due to blackouts.

Marines who have finished training display their discipline as they look to their next assignment.

"Remember when I was selling insurance and I tried to get you to take out a policy?"

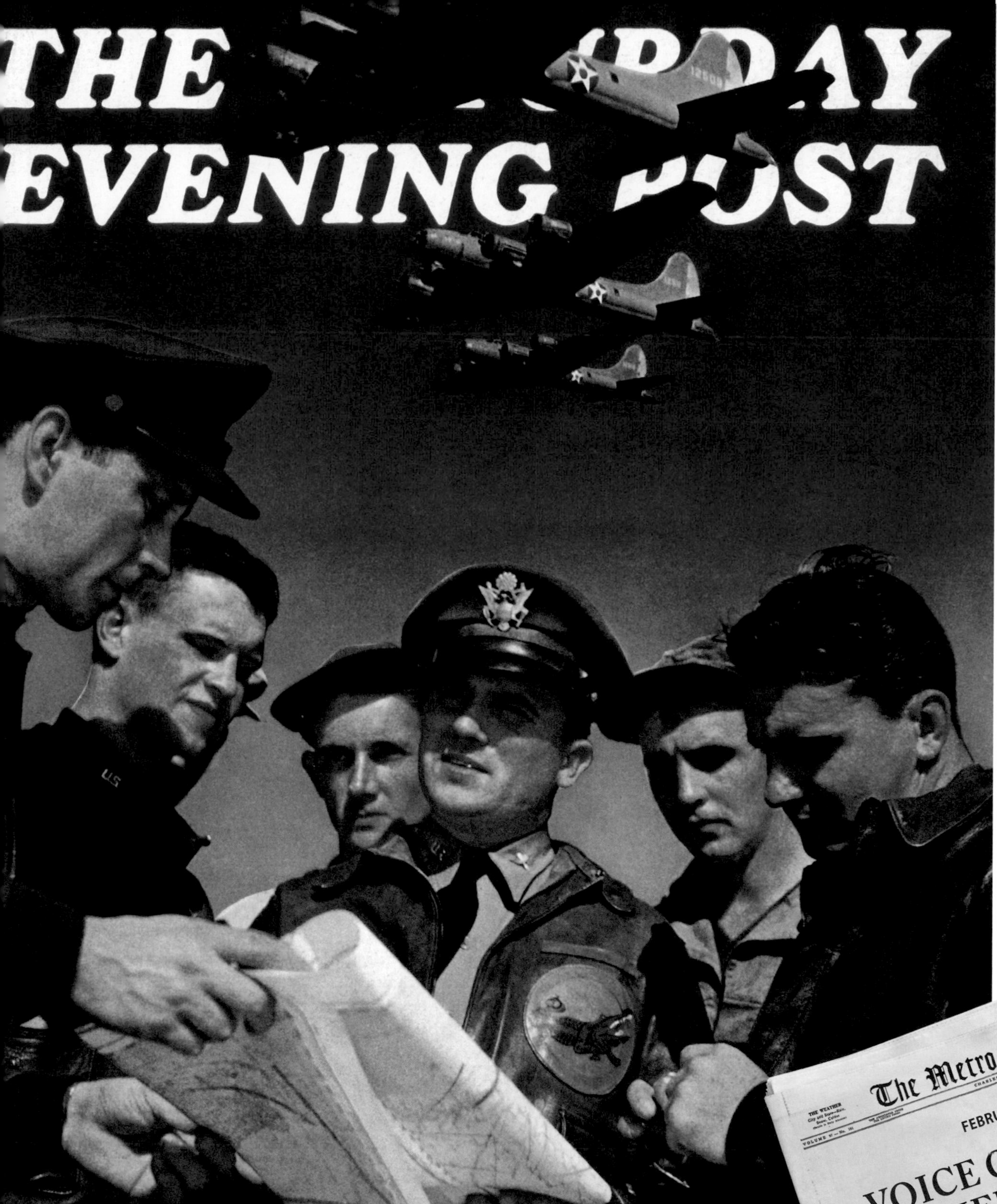

A group of flyers look over specified flight patterns in preparation for a strategic mission.

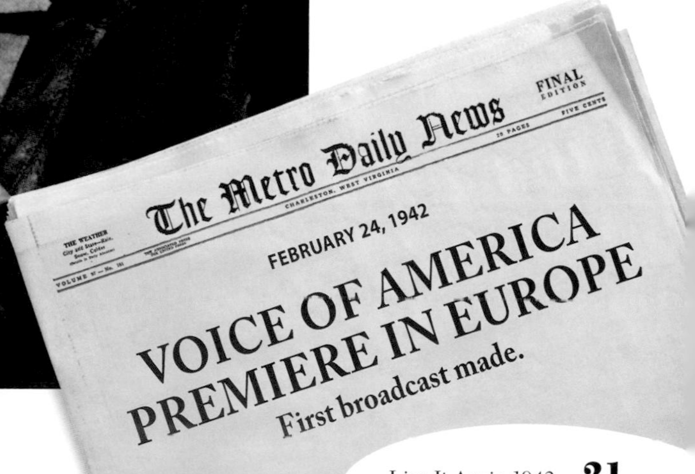

The Metro Daily News
CHARLESTON, WEST VIRGINIA
FINAL EDITION
FIVE CENTS
FEBRUARY 24, 1942
VOICE OF AMERICA PREMIERE IN EUROPE
First broadcast made.

Men Go to War

Rolling into battle

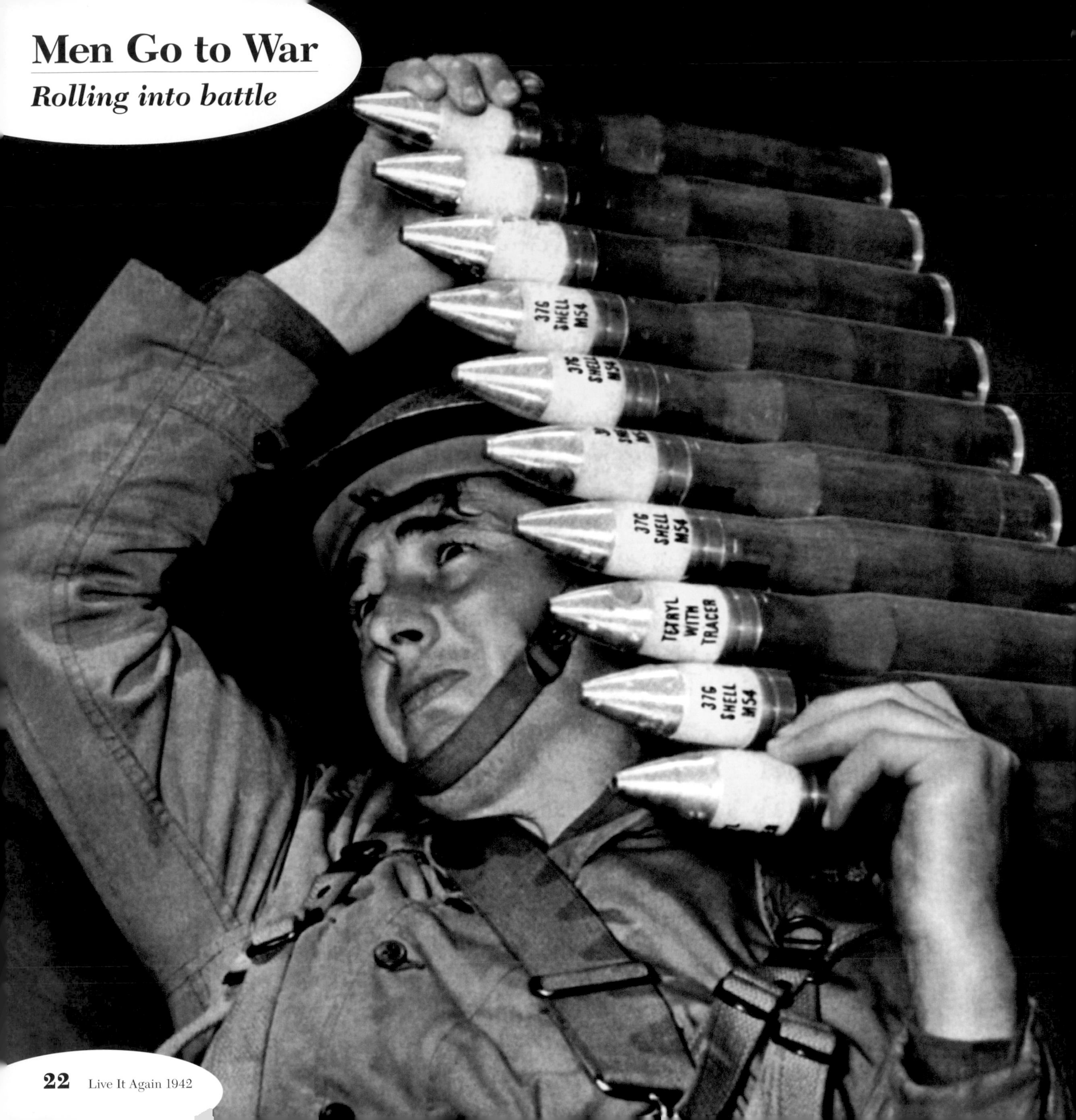
37G SHELL M54
37G SHELL M54
37G SHELL M54
TETRYL WITH TRACER
37G SHELL M54

Members of tank battalions frequently grew close as they had to rely on each other to effectively operate the large and unwieldy machines.

"Hope they send us a couple more messages by pigeon!"

During training, soldiers often had to learn to handle heavy artillery, like these M54 shells.

Soldiers signal their readiness as they form a line of tanks during a training session.

The Metro Daily News

FINAL EDITION

FEBRUARY 24-25, 1942

"BATTLE OF LOS ANGELES"

140 AA shells fired at unidentified slow moving object; no planes downed.

Everyday Life

From puppies to pigtails

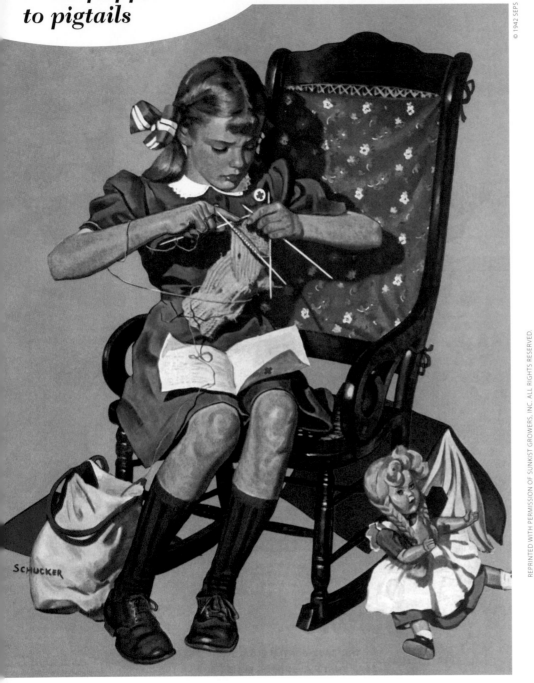

Spare moments were often filled with creativity such as knitting gifts in the comfort of Grandma's rocking chair.

"Gosh, he's in terrible shape—no hair, no teeth, nothing!"

Some things never change, including worried little children trying to find ways to hide a mistake by their favorite puppy.

© 1942 SEPS

"You better go back—somebody's got to tell them which way I went!"

Although giving the family pup a bath could be a big job, this pleased and pigtailed girl shows that she is up for the task.

The contribution of women proudly wearing their uniforms gradually overcame early prejudice against lady soldiers.

Women in Uniform

The idea of women in uniform began to take shape on May 14, 1942, when a bill was passed to establish a Women's Army Auxiliary Corps.

Though many servicemen were, no doubt, forced to swallow a little pride, it was just a matter of time before many were taking orders from women clad in suits representing the various branches of service.

By the time the war ended, 16 women had received Purple Hearts and 565 uniformed women had been awarded the Bronze Star for meritorious service overseas. Nurses received 1,619 citations and commendations of war for their service on the battlefields and on the war fronts.

The sight of wives in military uniforms seemed strange at first, but soon gained respect as women dedicated themselves to service.

Eloise Ellis, a supervisor at the Assembly of Repairs Department of the Naval Air Base in Corpus Christi, takes time to chat with one of the men.

rena Craig proudly rved as a cowler at the val Air Force Base in rpus Christi, Texas.

A uniformed Red Cross nurse takes a wishful glance at civilian fashions while heading towards duty in a World War II hot spot.

Gilbert Bundy

We Can Do It!

The perception that women were "weaker" than men was rapidly fading as ladies more than proved themselves capable of doing manual labor jobs while men were at war. Rosie the Riveter became a symbol of strength for women all over America.

POST FEB. 15 TO FEB. 28

WAR PRODUCTION CO-ORDINATING COMMIT

Women Go to Work

Keeping things going on the home front

While the men were away fighting for freedom, women stepped up to the plate to keep things going at home. From field work to industry, the ladies of the land stepped out of the home to assume new responsibilities.

With their hands firmly gripping farm machinery and factory tools, the ladies moved into the work world for a new role in the labor force.

In the early 1940s, it was becoming evident that role changes were taking place that would never return to the "old ways," even when the men returned from war.

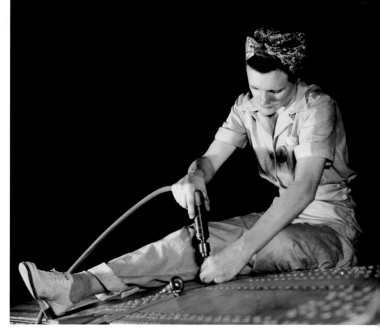

Women quickly caught on to the usage of tools and manual skills once thought to be the exclusive domain of the men of the community.

Whether riveting a tank or painting a wing, women were key to the success of the war effort at home and overseas.

Women Go to Work

In the factories

General Electric Women At War

Many women stepped into industrial jobs vacated by men to keep the lines moving making parts used overseas in war machinery.

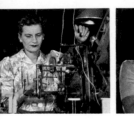

Women, like this electronics technician, were given the opportunity to learn and participate in professional trades generally considered to be "men's jobs" at the time.

Women expanded their traditional roles beyond nursing to work in research labs and other areas in medicine and technology.

Sewing skills learned in making clothes and repairing trousers were expanded to such tasks as making harnesses for parachutes and other war-use projects.

Women Join the *"Field Artillery"*

as International Harvester Dealers Teach Power Farming to an Army of "TRACTORETTES"

Up until the beginning of World War II, it was still generally perceived that a woman's place was in the home. However, as farmers were called to service, someone had to care for the harvest. In some cases, men would be deferred for that exact purpose, but most of the time, tradition was about to change forever as more women, like these "Tractorettes," learned to operate heavy farm equipment.

Farmers were thankful for the help of women who were willing to roll up their sleeves and head for the fields.

VICTORY WAITS ON YOUR FINGERS—

KEEP 'EM FLYING, MISS U.S.A.

UNCLE SAM NEEDS STENOGRAPHERS! • GET CIVIL SERVICE INFORMATION AT YOUR LOCAL POST OFFICE
U.S. CIVIL SERVICE COMMISSION, WASHINGTON, D.C.

The success of many wartime tactics was due to the supporting role of women carrying out their responsibilities on home soil.

Successful bombings in the heat of battle were due partly to the professional designs crafted by women who were trained to draft weapon architecture.

What Made Us Laugh

"Yes, sir; what can I do for you?"

"Now go in there and tell them you're lost . . .
I'll pick you up right after my defense meeting."

"All clear!"

"The generator went 'pfft, pfft' and then stopped!"

© 1942 SEPS

"Been doing anything exciting lately?"

© 1942 SEPS

"That will be all, Mrs. Beal. Thank you so much."

© 1942 SEPS

"I'm sorry, but the shock of your wanting a word from him has made your husband's spirit speechless."

© 1942 SEPS

"Somebody pulled the wool over his eyes."

Everyday Life

Sharing a moment

Reward... for a man who remembered !

© 1942 SEPS

"I'm warning you. You'll have to talk to her guardian first . . . she handles priorities."

Chocolate candy was the key that unlocked a woman's heart, especially when given by men who were returning from service in the military.

© 1942 SEPS

Nothing took away the loneliness of military service faster than the tender warmth of women welcoming those returning from overseas.

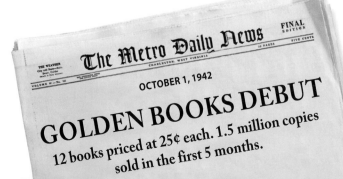

The Metro Daily News

FINAL EDITION

OCTOBER 1, 1942

GOLDEN BOOKS DEBUT

12 books priced at 25¢ each. 1.5 million copies sold in the first 5 months.

Proper formal attire was the custom of the day when going to a movie. Guys slicked down their hair and wore a suit, tie and vest while girls wore dresses and stylish hats.

There was no moment more meaningful than the one when a letter arrived from home. It represented the ultimate happiness for those serving in the military.

Hollywood Enlists

Inspiring a nation

When actor Jimmy Stewart became one of the first movie stars to enlist in the service, he initiated a trend that won the admiration of both civilians and soldiers.

Stewart's efforts were not only successful, but he ended the war with 20 combat missions and remained in the Air Force where he was later promoted to Brigadier General.

Within a short time, other stars also enlisted. Clark Gable, in particular, was often followed by MGM photographers who grabbed opportunities of service moments to use as clips in war movies at the time.

News of the stars' enlistments spread around the world and became a morale-booster to U.S. troops.

Jimmy Stewart was already a trained pilot when he enlisted in the Army Air Corps. During his military career, he received several prestigious military honors, including the famed French Air Force award, *Croix de Guerre.*

Lieutenant Jimmy Stewart, clad in his uniform, displayed his early involvement in the war and inspired America during his address to the Oscars where he accepted the best actor award for his role in the 1940 movie, *The Philadelphia Story*. Stewart, an early recruit as an instructor, saw active combat during the final years of World War II and eventually rose to the rank of Brigadier General. In January of 1942 Stewart earned a commission as a second lieutenant and was posted to Moffett Field as an instructor pilot.

Hollywood Enlists

Across the services

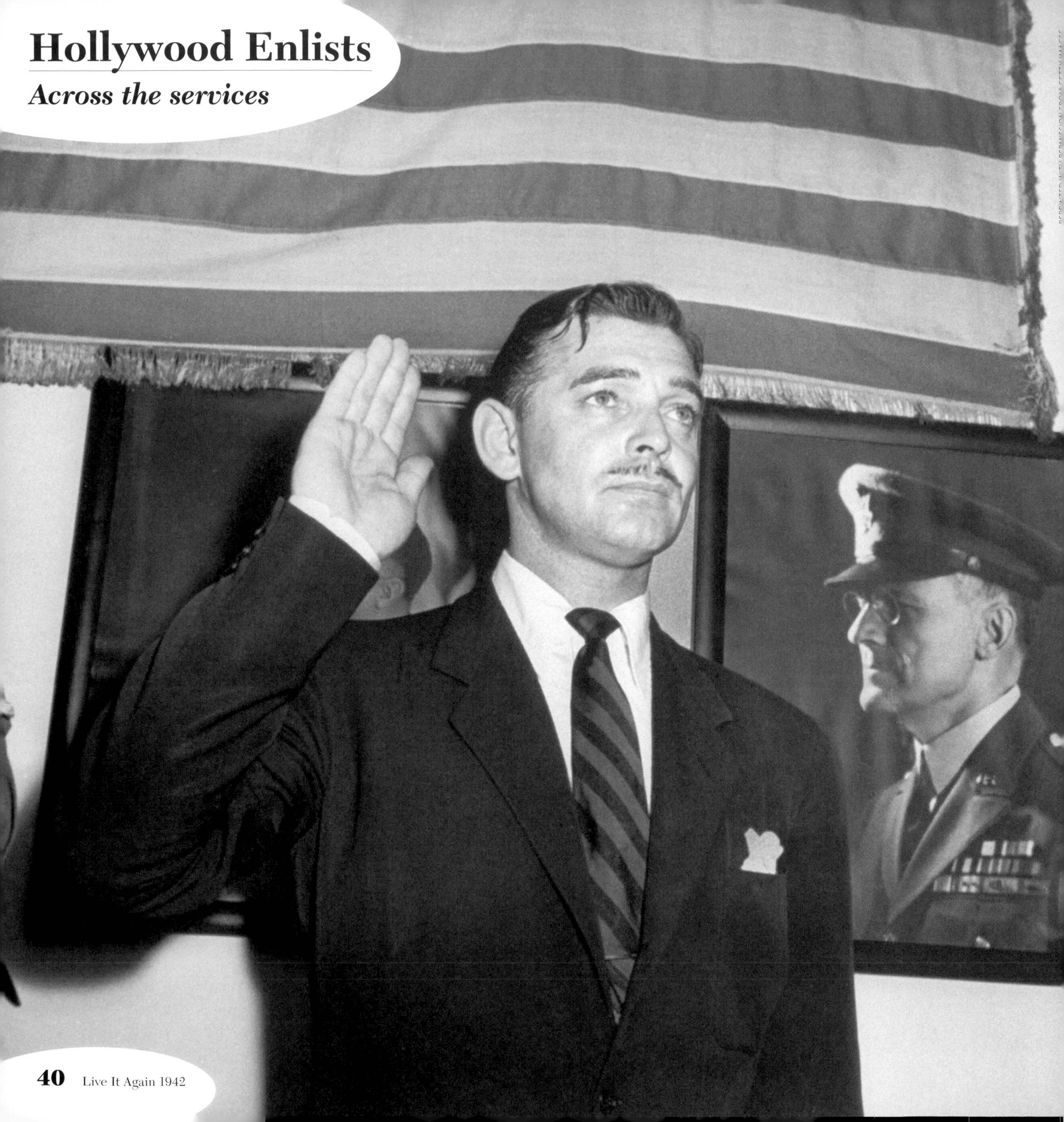

Despite being beyond the age of the draft, actor Clark Gable enlisted as a private in the United States Army Air Forces training school on August 12, 1942 at Los Angeles. After graduating later that year as a second lieutenant, he attended gunnery school and was assigned to the 351st Bomb Group at Polebrook, England. From there he flew operational missions over Europe in B-17's.

I WANT YOU

Actor **Audie Murphy** enlisted in the Army in 1942 at age 16 with birth records his sister falsified. Murphy was originally rejected by the Marines as being too short at 5' 5." Audie later became one of the most decorated servicemen of World War II, receiving 33 awards and commendations, including the highest award possible, the Medal of Honor. Murphy's exposure from the notoriety of his military career led to his success in Hollywood.

Clark Gable graduated from the United States Army Air Force training on Oct. 28, 1942. Class members selected him as graduation speaker.

STARS WHO ENLISTED IN 1942

Gene Autry, Air Force
Eddie Albert, Navy
Robert Cummings, Army Air Corps.
Henry Fonda, Navy
Glenn Ford, Marines
Russell Johnson, Army
Walter Matthau, Air Force
Glenn Miller, Air Force
Tyrone Power, Marines
John Russell, Marines
William Talman, Army
Jack Warden, Army/Paratrooper

Lieutenant Jimmy Steward and Captain Clark Gable on leave in Hollywood.

HISTORY.SANDIEGO.EDU/CDR2/WW2PICS2/82624

Clark Gable was photographed while he was a member of the 8th Air Force B-17 in Britain. Gable joined the United States Army Air Forces following the tragic death of his wife, Carole Lombard, in 1942.

"Why can't they just let us be lonesome?"

USO

Serving the troops

The United Service Organizations (USO) established its overseas department in January of 1942 in order to set up entertainment clubs outside the continental United States.

Almost immediately, Bob Hope utilized the organization to broadcast entertainment programs to the Armed Forces. Hope was so moved by the sacrifices of the U.S. troops that he and his radio troupe traveled weekly to perform, "The Pepsodent Show," on military training sites.

Soon entertainers, led by Bob Hope, were travelling to USO locations all over the world to entertain the troops.

Soldiers and civilians merged at USO service clubs for dancing, movies and other types of entertainment. Clubs served as a bridge between the public and the military.

Bob Hope, with friends like Frances Langford, quickly utilized the USO to entertain those making huge sacrifices on behalf of the United States.

Things lightened quickly for military personnel when they indulged in coffee and doughnuts served up by volunteers from the USO during a break in the action.

After delivering a speech to ship builders emphasizing the importance of their role in winning the war, actor and singer Paul Robeson leads them in singing "The Star Spangled Banner."

Musicians like Earl (Fatha) Hines, leader of the Hines Orchestra, often performed for servicemen.

Boxers Jackie Wilson and Ray Robinson, normally opponents in the ring, fought side-by-side once they enlisted for the same unit.

African-Americans Enter the Service

Entertainers

It wasn't easy, but African-American entertainers broke into the service arena by reaching out to U.S. troops fighting in World War II.

President Franklin Roosevelt and First Lady Eleanor Roosevelt quickly embraced and promoted their efforts to entertain and inspire the troops.

Contralto singer Marian Anderson fought the barriers of racial prejudice to take her show to those in military service in 1942 performances.

Hattie McDaniel (in dark suit in the front row), Chairman of the Negro Division of the Hollywood Victory Committee, leads a troop of entertainers to perform for servicemen. She was the first African-American to win an Academy Award. She won Best Actress in a Supporting Role for her role as "Mammy" in *Gone with the Wind*.

African-Americans Enter the Service

Military firsts

Ruth C. Isaacs, Katherine Horton and Inez Patterson are among the first African-American WAVES to enter service.

William Baldwin, the first African-American Navy recruit for general service, was sworn in on June 2, 1942.

Charity Adams, who enlisted in the Women's Army Auxiliary Corps in July 1942, was the first African-American woman to be commissioned as an officer.

Phyllis Mae Dailey (second from right), the Navy's first African-American nurse, is one of five Navy nurses commissioned in New York. By 1942, large numbers of African-American women were volunteering for service.

...ward Perry was the ...t African-American to ...list in the U.S. Marine ...rps. The Marines ...rted enlisting ...rican-Americans on ...e 1, 1942.

The first African-American members of the Women's Army Corps assigned overseas stand for inspection.

2335 Norwalk Avenue,
Los Angeles, Calif.
Sept. 12, 1942

The Commandant,
United States Marine Corps,
Washington, D.C.

Dear Sir:

I desire enlistment in the Marine Corps Reserve, Class 5-B, Specialist, to serve in the capacity of training and direction of Navajo Indian personnel for communication, and to perform duty with them both inside and outside the limits of continental United States; with non-commissioned rank commensurate with duties assigned.

Your authority for my induction into the service is requested. The basis for this request is as follows:

Twenty-two years of residence among the Navajo Indians, starting when I was four years of age, enabled me to become fluent in the language of this tribe. At the age of nine, I acted as interpreter for President Theodore Roosevelt at the White House; and subsequently, on many occasions, as court interpreter in Arizona. Since establishing my residence here, I have continued my use of the language through frequent visits to the reservation, and lecture work (see inclosed circular).

Last February, it occurred to me that the Navajo language might be ideally suited to use by the Marine Corps for code in oral communication. I presented this idea to Lieutenant Colonel (then Major) J.E. Jones, Force Communication Officer at Camp Elliott, who agreed the plan was worth considering. I offered to make a search in Los Angeles for enough Navajos to permit a practical demonstration, and Colonel Jones accepted my offer. Two days after my return to this city, I received a letter from him, stating that General Vogel was interested, and requesting further information. A copy of his letter, and the report I prepared in compliance therewith, are inclosed.

On February 27th, I arrived at Camp Elliott with four Navajos; a fifth had been located in the Naval service at San Diego and brought to Camp Elliott. The following morning at 8:15, Colonel Jones gave me six typical messages used in military operations, and asked me to report at Divisional Headquarters at nine o'clock for the demonstration. These messages contained many terms for which no equivalents exist in the Navajo language, and we had only a short time to devise such terms.

The demonstration was held as scheduled, in the presence of General Clayton B. Vogel and his staff. Its results and the General's verdict are summarized in the communication sent by him to your office on March 5th.

Mr. Philip Johnston's letter to the Commandant of the Marine Corps.

Code Talkers Save the War Effort in the Pacific

In early 1942, Philip Johnston, son of a missionary to the Navajos in Arizona, met with Major General Clayton B. Vogel, commanding general of the Amphibious Corps, Pacific Fleet.

Johnston discussed with Vogel the possibility of utilizing the Navajo language as a code for Pacific Theater. An extremely complex, unwritten language without alphabet or symbols, it is virtually unknown outside the Navajo nation.

Once trained, Navajo code talkers transmitted orders, plus information on tactics, troop movements and other vital battlefield communications over telephones and radios.

The Japanese were never able to break the code.

UNITED STATES MARINE CORPS

NARA

UNITED STATES MARINE CORPS

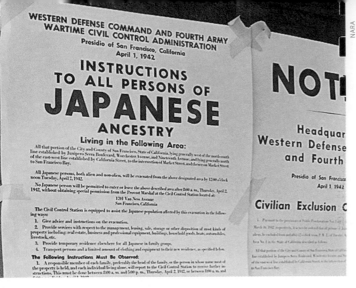

Instructions were issued governing the regulations of those who had been moved from their homes to special living quarters.

Japanese-Americans arrive at the train station near the San Pedro Internment camp.

Japanese-Americans Relocated

On Feb. 19, 1942, on the heels of the Japanese attack on Pearl Harbor, President Franklin Roosevelt issued an executive order which forced 120,000 Japanese Americans into "relocation camps."

The order was based on the suspicion that the Japanese military was preparing a full-scale attack on the west coast of the United States and the fear that some in the U.S. Japanese community might be spies for the Japanese government.

One of the most noted sites was the Manzanar Relocation Center. In 1942, the U.S. Army leased 6,200 acres from Los Angeles to establish this site to hold Japanese-Americans during World War II.

Manzanar was later established as a national historic site to serve as a reminder to future generations of these fragile times.

Harvesting the crop at th
Manzanar Relocation Cente

A Japanese-American family awaits evacuation as part of presidential orders authorizing military commanders to move Japanese families at their discretion.

The Metro Daily News

FDR SIGNS EXECUTIVE ORDER 9066

On Feb. 19, 1942, Roosevelt issues executive order authorizing military commanders to designate military areas for relocation of Japanese Americans.

MEAD
SCHAEFFER

The Sullivan brothers became instant celebrities when this photo of the five was circulated widely and became the symbol of an entire family's commitment from the heartland to defend our country. Photographers captured this family-centered, patriotic moment prior to one of the most tragic events of the Pacific theater. On November 13, 1942, all five Sullivan brothers died when the USS Juneau sank.

The Metro Daily News

FINAL EDITION

THE WEATHER
City and State skies
Snow, Colder
March 2, Daily Edition

VOLUME 57 — No. 151
CHARLESTON, WEST VIRGINIA

IV PAGES

FIVE CENTS

JUNE 4, 1942

STUNNING U.S. VICTORY
BATTLE OF MIDWAY
Will prove to be a turning point in the Pacific.

War in the Pacific

The war in the Pacific brought out the most devastating events possible, but it also had moments lending themselves to adrenalin-filled human elation.

Aug. 7, 1942 was a significant date in the war in the Pacific. Alexander A. Vandegrift's First Marine Division took the Japanese garrison by surprise at Guadalcanal. They overran Henderson Field, the island's landing strip, and engaged in the conflict known as, "Bloody Ridge."

Theater operations led to other important conflicts such as the Battle of Midway where the work of American code breakers enabled the United States Navy to decisively defeat the Imperial Japanese Navy; this was one of the turning points of the Pacific Theater.

"He has a plan to sink the Jap navy, sir."

This official U.S. Coast Guard painting depicts Douglas Munro's last moments while evacuating Marines at Guadalcanal. He was the only member of the Coast Guard to receive the Medal of Honor.

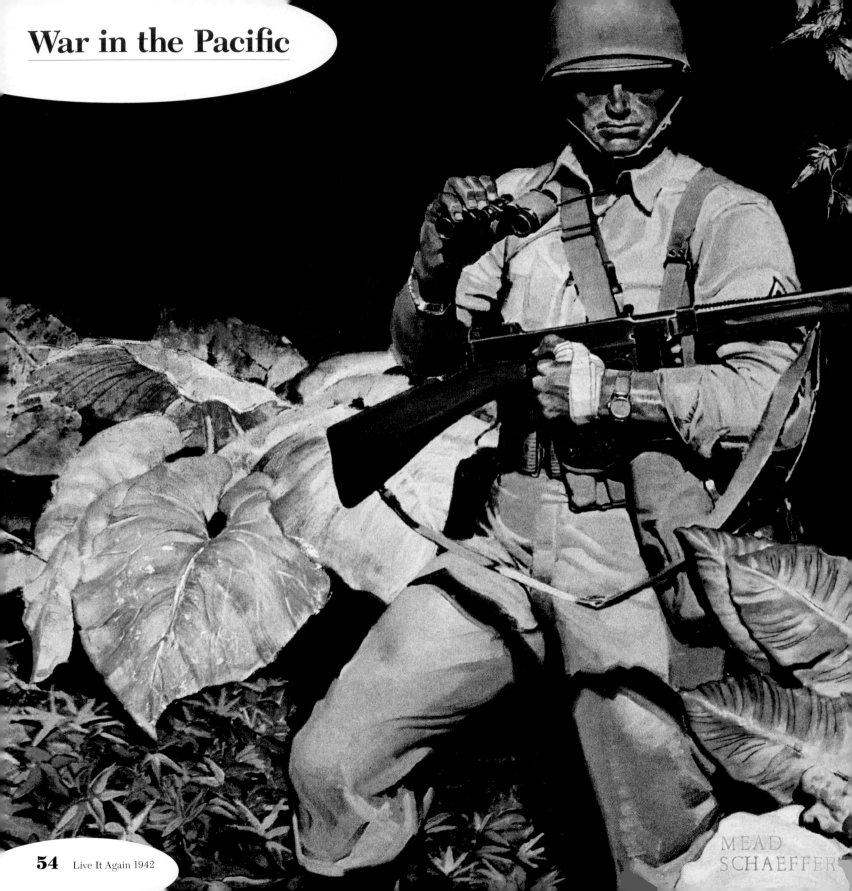

MEAD
SCHAEFFER

On Aug. 7, 1942, Major General Alexander Vandegrift led the 1st Marine Division in the first major offensive against the Japanese at the Solomon Islands. Vandegrift was later awarded the Navy Cross. Here, he appears with Richmond Turner aboard the USS McCawley.

(Above) Lieutenant Colonel Bill Whaling was photographed with his troops on Guadalcanal in September. (Below) Fresh troops from the 2nd Marine Division take a break during a halt in the action on Guadalcanal.

A United States Marine patrol crosses the Matanikau River on Guadalcanal in September of 1942.

THE WEATHER
City and Scene Fair.
Snow. Colder
Rising a bit warmer.

The Metro Daily News

VOLUME 87 — No. 161

FINAL EDITION

20 PAGES   FIVE CENTS

CHARLESTON, WEST VIRGINIA

MARCH 1942

GENERAL MACARTHUR LEAVES PHILIPINES

He utters famous phrase, "I shall return."

What Made Us Laugh

"It's all right—they're with me."

"Let's change the subject—let's talk about brunettes for a while!"

"What kind of message is this from Von Klieg—
'We have met the enemy and we are theirs'?"

"Word of honor, mom—as <u>soon</u> as I need it I'll send for it."

"It's our class in Civilian Hazards—for men going on furlough."

"But we're going to a <u>formal</u> party.
Where's your gold braid and sword?"

"Oliver hasn't quite got the hang of it!"

The Home Front
Hopes, comforts & challenges

"Well, as I was saying ——"

"If My Mess Sergeant Could Only See Me Now!"

The Promise of the Sky

Model airplanes based on World War II aircraft became the rage of the time during and right after World War II. Their meaning was especially enhanced when they were replicas of those flown by family members and friends.

After eating food interpretations of all kinds of wartime cooks, the refrigerator at home looked pretty good to soldiers who returned to their favorite cakes, pies, cookies and snacks. The temptation to indulge was overwhelming for homesick appetites enjoying home cooking again.

Norman Rockwell's fictional character, Willis Gillis, Jr., became a friend to many American households who "met" Gillis on the cover of the *The Saturday Evening Post* during World War II. Rockwell's portrayals of Gillis represented "every man" and concerns about the war. Here, Gillis and his fictional girlfriend touch on the matter of blackouts in this painting that appeared on the cover of the June 27, 1942, Post.

WHAT TO DO IN A BLACKOUT

Norman Rockwell

THE WEATHER
City and State—Rain.

The Metro Daily News

FINAL
EDITION

VOLUME 41 — No. 101

CHARLESTON, WEST VIRGINIA

20 PAGES

FIVE CENTS

REVENUE ACT OF 1942
Largest tax increase in U.S. history, increasing rates and quadrupling the number of tax payers.

© 1942 SEPS

"Patsy'll get the car, Eleanor'll bring the tires, you bring the gas and I'll bring the potato salad."

Rationing

A new way of life

Following the Japanese attack on Pearl Harbor, the economy took a sudden turn from domestic to war production, leaving Americans scrambling in a new system of rationing and cutbacks.

A government-imposed system of war ration books, stamps and tokens were quickly issued regulating the usage of such goods as sugar, meat, silk, shoes, nylon and many other popular store-bought items.

Perhaps, nothing affected the lives of Americans more than the rationing of gasoline. Casual driving was limited to what could be undertaken with a four-gallon purchase a week while eight gallons was tops for the most necessary driving.

Ration stamps were a hot commodity in 1942. Owners who lost them or had them stolen often found themselves struggling to put food on the table.

RATION BOOK HOLDER

No. 407356EA
United States of America
Office of Price Administration

WAR RATION BOOK FOUR

4

Issued to

Complete address

READ BEFORE SIGNING

THE WEATHER
City and State—Rain
Snow, Colder

VOLUME 87 — No. 143

The Metro Daily News

CHARLESTON, WEST VIRGINIA

FINAL
EDITION

FIVE CENTS

MAY 1942

SUGAR RATIONING BEGINS

Many Americans turn sour.

HOWARD SCOTT

Rationing

A new shopping experience

In games, such as Monopoly, spinners often replaced dice due to rationing of certain products.

RATIONING MEANS A FAIR SHARE FOR ALL OF US

Cartoons often communicated reasoning for certain government actions. This sketch shows the fact that rationing was administered so each family would get its fair share of products and food in short supply due to military needs or import reductions.

Food rationing often caused purchasers to do special planning in order to comply with regulations related to everyday grocery items.

Acquiring rationing coupons often involved long lines and timely planning on behalf of those seeking to secure ration distributions. In spite of attempts to keep the program fair, scams were common and watched closely by government officials.

To aid the public and keep people informed, several businesses published a monthly "ration calendar" showing the status of many categories of goods. The worth of stamps would often change on a daily basis.

Rationing
Supporting the war effort

Initial attempts at volunteer fuel rationing failed. Here, cars line up to purchase gasoline in Washington D.C. on July 21, 1942, the day before stricter gas rationing went into effect.

Do with less—so <u>they'll</u> have enough!

RATIONING GIVES YOU YOUR FAIR SHARE

TEANECK 2 GALLONS

MEADVILLE 1 GALLON

GEORGE WOLFE

The Metro Daily News

FINAL EDITION

DECEMBER 1942

GAS RATIONING BEGINS
Americans get stranded.

America was quickly termed as "the sleepy nation" when rationing limited the amount of coffee that could be purchased. Although the goal of rationing was to allow for fair distribution without favoritism among all financial classes, counterfeiting and black market operations remained critical problems within the system. On the positive side, many close-knit communities also found ways to share products among themselves.

Even government officials had to follow rationing guidelines. In this photo, the administrator of the Office of Price Administration's wife has to sign up for her sugar quota.

Family members were given their own ration book and were responsible for properly using them and keeping them in a safe place. Here a young boy uses his ration book to make a purchase.

Children of the time acted out domestic life as they knew it. In 1942, it was not unusual for children to set up a rationing play store, complete with details and records, to reflect what they were witnessing in the practices of their families. In many cases, such practices enabled the young people to better understand the economics of the war.

HOWARD
SCOTT

Recycling

Everybody pitches in

For a generation transitioning from the Great Depression to the heartache of war, salvaging second-hand items was a way of discovering recyclable treasures and doing one's part by donating salvage items for military use.

Tires were fished out of ponds and confiscated from salvage yards. Families walked along railroad tracks to retrieve coal that had fallen off the train or to pick wild strawberries for fresh preserves.

Fathers would take their sons to salvage yards to look for items that could be reconditioned into something useful at home or for a salvage drive. Grandmothers and grandchildren would save old material to cut into quilt blocks and comforters.

Perhaps the most valuable treasure in all of this was friends and families working together to restore items for use. That spirit of recycling was not only joyfully competitive, at times, but initiated hope in the midst of the sagging spirits of wartime.

"*Some people have all the luck. All I've been gettin' is fish.*"

ARCHIVES NATIONALS DU QUEBEC

There was a sense of satisfaction when children found items, like tires and boots made of recyclable rubber, that made valuable and patriotic donations.

Many clubs and societies sponsored scrap and salvage drives so everyone, from children to adults, had a way to pitch in to help the war effort.

Recycling

Hollywood does its part

Singer Bing Crosby was one of many celebrities that took the lead in recycling during World War II. Here, Crosby is pictured salvaging golf balls for a scrap rubber drive to replace rubber being utilized in the war effort.

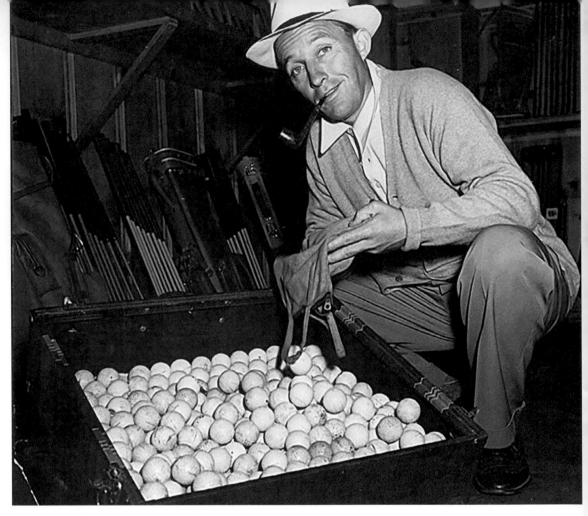

Rita Hayworth lent her star power to the effort appealing to everyone to get involved and follow her example by making their own donation.

PLEASE DRIVE CAREFULLY, MY BUMPERS ARE ON THE SCRAP HEAP

"I deliver 'em in the morning and salvage 'em in the afternoon."

Salvaging was so critically important, both for use in war construction and to replace products used for World War II needs. People were saving everything from bacon grease to various rubber-based products to donate for war use. The publicity stirred by stars, such as Bing Crosby and Rita Hayworth, went a long way in motivating the nation, and especially its young people, to recycle and distribute products made rare by war usage.

Even non-celebrities became stars of their own scrap drives. Here, office worker Annette del Sur shows off some of the metal scrap collected at her work place, the Douglas Aircraft Company.

Recycling
Everything gets a second chance

Products such as rubber and silk were especially needed because the Japanese had cut off the supply by their rapid advance through southeast Asia.

"Malcolm and I feel that our tire problem will soon be solved."

The government sought to instill in Americans their patriotic duty to contribute recyclable items to the war effort with posters like this.

YOUR SCRAP
...brought it down

KEEP SCRAPPING
Rubber · Metal · Rag

GIVE TO A COLLECTOR, SALVAGE DEPOT OR SELL TO A DEALER

Scrap carts were placed at various neighborhood drop-off points to collect a variety of items to be used in World War II construction.

Not only were children taught at home the benefits of collecting scrap, but they were also shown at school how they could help the war effort. Many students brought in scrap metal and used tires to school collection sites. Others even contributed their own toys for scrap metal drives.

"You're permitted a ten-second dip."

The government organized major recycling efforts setting goals by state. Here, a contingent of representatives from Virginia proudly display their contribution in front of the United States Capitol.

Women would gather together to repair potential recyclables for future use. Quite often the repair sessions would become a social time, complete with carry-in meals and home-made baked goods.

People were discouraged from buying new tires and were prompted to instead "save" their tires by having them recapped.

Conservation Nation

Conserving was nothing new to many Americans

The conservation needed to cope with World War II rationing was nothing new to many Americans who, just a decade earlier, had learned to cope with the demands of the Great Depression.

Those in rural areas continued to process their own vegetables, although in many cases it was wives left behind that farmed gardens and orchards. Everybody had conservation drawers filled with salvaged paper clips, rubber bands, pencils, envelopes, crayons, can lids and many other reusable items. Perhaps one of the most regulated commodities was gas, which Americans conserved by carpooling.

In a time before it carried a negative connotation, hitchhiking became a way of life for families going shopping, looking for a way to a special event or needing rides to work. Family members would pack lunches for the day's activity; even the family dog occasionally got in on the activity.

It's the patriotic gesture now!

Doublin' Up...

THESE DAYS, WITH CARS SO <u>IMPORTANT</u>, MORE AND MORE FOLKS SEE ME REGULARLY, TO MAKE THEIR CARS LAST.

Your Mobilgas Dealer

© 1942 SEPS

Carpooling was often the solution for those going to common destinations such as school activities, work or church. Many companies recognized the need for Americans to "make their cars last." No new cars were being built as all resources were directed to the war effort.

"They'll be a little late this morning. Mr. Watson's car just broke down."

What Made Us laugh

"I don't know what you're complaining about, Malcolm. Of all the men who take me out, *you're* the only one I'm *engaged* to."

"I passed in everything except conduct— but I'll never use *that* outside of school."

"Yes, I know Tommy's waiting—but I dressed quicker than I thought."

"George is so inconsistent—no matter how many times I change my mind, he always agrees with me."

"I don't believe that new accountant will be with us much longer."

"Well, then, will you ask Mr. Thorneton to step out here for a moment? I'm sure if he saw me, he'd see me!"

"Well, since you put it that way—I don't know."

"Wanta see me make a guy superstitious?"

Everyday Life
Those darn kids

Norman Rockwell

It was one thing to snoop in a sister's room, but this boy carried it one step further when he discovered her diary and found amusement in its contents. The March 21, 1942, cover of *The Saturday Evening Post* was a classic example of how artist Norman Rockwell sought to capture everyday life in America while the nation was nervous about the war going on around it.

The Metro Daily News

FINAL EDITION

THE WEATHER
City and State—Rain,
Snow, Colder

CHARLESTON, WEST VIRGINIA, MONDAY EVENING, DECEMBER 9, 1941

FIVE CENTS

JUNE 13 & 17, 1942

FBI CAPTURES 8 GERMAN MARINES FROM U-BOATS
Germans came ashore off Long Island and Florida.

Ready for mischief, this little boy can't wait to scare his anxiously awaiting sister with the loud crack of his balloon.

"Dear, I wish you'd talk to our daughter here. She's a gun moll for that poolroom mob."

"He practic'ly proposed—he told me he wanted to marry a girl with brains!"

These young men, who think they are getting away with something, fall under the watchful eye of the coat check woman.

The purchase of war bonds was promoted as a show of patriotism. Posters encouraged raising money for World War II as a way for family members and friends to help those who had placed their lives in jeopardy on behalf of the American public.

Much of the advertising about bond sales used visual images of war machinery under construction, thanks to assistance from Americans. Several photographs of ships under construction were marketed as a reminder of support needed to purchase supplies.

BUY WAR BONDS

Involving the entire family in saving money to purchase bonds became an attractive way of families unifying to support the military effort while teaching children to be unselfish in giving toward important causes such as the war.

War Bonds

Sales boost national spirits

The concept of purchasing war bonds to assist with military expenses appealed to many Americans as a way to lend their support to World War II financial needs.

Bond rallies were held all over the country, often supported by famous singers or Hollywood stars. The "Stars Over America" blitz raised a total of $838,540,000.

Another popular method of raising money through war bonds involved a card with 75 quarter slots that would total $18.75. Once it was full, it could be turned into the post office for a $25 war bond that matured in 10 years.

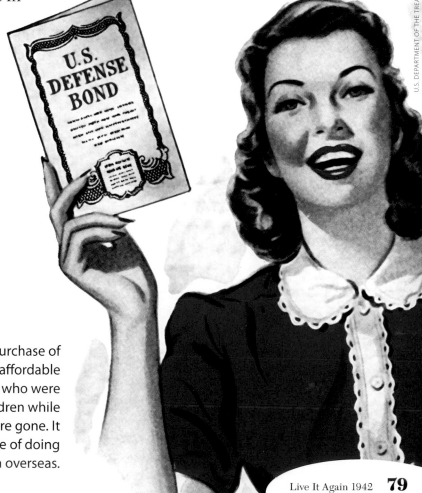

WANTED - *FIGHTING DOLLARS*

MAKE EVERY PAY-DAY BOND-DAY

UNITED STATES DEFENSE BONDS · STAMPS

Ask about our payroll savings plan

The incorporation of purchasing bonds through payroll enabled many workers to donate bond money through their places of work and other meaningful sources.

U.S. DEFENSE BOND

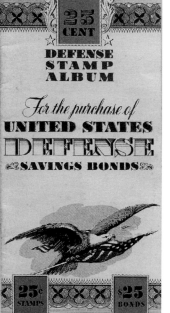

25 CENT

DEFENSE STAMP ALBUM

For the purchase of

UNITED STATES DEFENSE SAVINGS BONDS

25¢ STAMPS $25 BONDS

The method of purchasing 25 cent stamps to build the worth of a United States bond became attractive to children and members of the American work force who couldn't afford to purchase bonds with larger amounts of money.

Various options for purchase of war bonds made them affordable for mothers at home who were taking care of their children while their husbands were gone. It gave women a sense of doing something for their men overseas.

BUY

A SHARE IN AMERICA

FOR DEE

BABE SAYS:

What had once been known as "baby bonds" were marketed by the treasury as "defense bonds" in order to raise funds for the war effort.

BUY the New VICTORY BONDS

Don't Let That Shadow Touch Them
Buy WAR BONDS

A popular marketing strategy to encourage Americans to purchase bonds was to remind them of the dangers that losing ground could place on children. The appeal to maintaining family safety by winning the war was all it took for many Americans to invest in the purchase of war bonds.

WARNING!
OUR HOMES ARE IN DANGER NOW!
OUR JOB KEEP 'EM FIRING

"you buy 'em we'll fly 'em!"

DEFENSE BONDS STAMPS

THE MORE BONDS YOU BUY—THE MORE PLANES WE'LL FLY

One of the simplest ways to invest in war bonds was by purchasing defense bonds stamps. Money raised by the bonds purchased all types of war equipment, including fighter planes.

Victory Gardens

Strengthening family roots

Advertisements in magazines promoted the nutritional benefits of producing one's own fruit and vegetables.

In addition to shortages of rationed foods, vegetable shortages developed at many markets, especially in urban areas.

In order to replace those vegetables, the government made an all-out effort to encourage American families to grow their own vegetables in a "Victory Garden."

Although the concept represented a way of life for many rural families, it was entirely different for families living in urban areas. Vegetable gardens started popping up in places where they had never been seen before, including roofs, front yards and recycled flower gardens.

At one point, it was estimated that nearly 20 million Americans had adopted the practice of growing their own fruits and vegetables.

When fresh fruit and vegetables became scarce at local markets, Americans were encouraged to grow, save and store their own produce.

THE SATURDAY EVENING POST

Even a small garden could be a big help to both a family and its country by contributing to the dwindling supply of fresh fruits and vegetables.

Victory Gardens

Keep America strong

With many of the young farmers serving in the war, those left behind to care for the crops were deeply valued. In some cases, the U.S. Army assigned farmers back to their fields, especially for crops in short supply such as beets and various grains. Many farmers worked in teams to protect the physical well-beings of each other.

FAMOUS BIRTHDAYS
Harrison Ford, July 13 Actor

There was a strong emphasis on nutritional eating to promote good health and strength to carry on the tasks at home. Government sponsored "U.S. needs US strong" advertisements stressed the importance of healthy eating.

EAT FRUITS & VEGETABLES

U.S. NEEDS US STRONG

EAT NUTRITIONAL FOOD

DO YOUR PART IN THE NATIONAL NUTRITION PROGRAM

Office of Defense Health and Welfare Services, Washington, D.C.

Plenty of sleep
keeps him on the job

Fun, off the job
keeps him on the job

Foods that count
keep him on the job

Cartoons promoted fostering good health habits such as plenty of rest, time for relaxation and nutritional eating to deal with the stresses and hard work caused by the reduction in the work force.

Everyday Life
Everyday foods

"I'm all for this
COFFEE THAT GIVES DOUBLE PLEASURE!"

Save up to 25%
ON MANY FINE FOODS

*Many A&P brands (sold only at A&P) bring you savings up to 25% compared to prices usually asked for other nationally known products of comparable quality. You'll enjoy the goodness of our—

33 Ann Page Foods
White House Evaporated Milk
Eight O'Clock, Red Circle and Bokar Coffees
Marvel "Enriched" Bread
Jane Parker Cakes, Rolls and "Dated" Donuts
A&P Canned Fruits and Vegetables

Nectar and Our Own Teas
Sunnyfield Butter
Mel-O-Bit Cheese
White Sail Household Products
7 Sunnyfield Cereals
Sunnyfield Hams and Smoked Meats
Sunnyfield Flours
and many other fine foods

© 1942—The Great Atlantic & Pacific Tea Co.

Eight O'Clock coffee was a very popular brand in 1942. Coffee was promoted as a nice accompaniment to a shared moment or a time spent alone reading a letter from a husband away at war.

Kellogg's Rice Krispies was often promoted as the "talking cereal." Advertisements touted that the cereal had Uncle Sam's stamp of approval, thus connecting sentimentally with patriotism.

Crisp
so crisp they "talk"!
snap! crackle! pop!

U.S. NEEDS US STRONG
THIS TYPE OF FOOD IS AMONG THOSE RECOMMENDED IN THE NUTRITION FOOD RULES
EAT NUTRITIONAL FOOD

Whole grain nutritive values, too . . . the kind Uncle Sam recommends!

ALL *Kellogg* CEREALS are made from WHOLE GRAIN or are restored to WHOLE GRAIN VALUES in thiamin, niacin and iron as recommended by the U.S. NUTRITION FOOD RULES

Kellogg's RICE KRISPIES

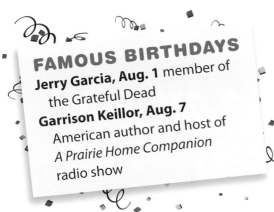

The August 22nd *The Saturday Evening Post* bore the cover known as "The Biggest Watermelon." Almost immediately, the cover image and the magazine became a collector's item.

THE SATURDAY EVENING

POST

August 22, 1942   10¢

A COMPLETE NOVEL

SO DEEP MY LOVE

—

Rough-on-Japs Doolittle

"Just between us girls..."

Let's admit we can't make vegetable soup any better than Campbell's!"

Campbell's Vegetable Soup

With the absence of many husbands, household chores fell more heavily on wives and mothers. Soup became associated with a quicker way to prepare a nutritious meal for family members.

The Metro Daily News

FINAL EDITION

AUGUST 9, 1942

NEW YORK TIMES PUBLISHES FIRST BESTSELLER LIST

Disclosure of the slightest bit of information could be fatal or cause loss in certain military operations. The smallest slip of the tongue could force a change in military strategy, cause injury to fellow comrades and even lead to loss of life.

HE'S WATCHING YOU

Those in military service were cautioned to never talk about classified information in public. Even certain body language movements were considered potentially fatal if noticed by trained enemy observers.

I'M COUNTING ON YOU!

DON'T DISCUSS:
TROOP MOVEMENTS
SHIP SAILINGS · WAR EQUIPMENT

Loose Lips Sink Ships

A slip of the tongue could be fatal

Most Americans entering military service had no comprehension of how the disclosure of one key piece of information could play into the enemy's hand. One of the first aspects of military training was how to conduct one's self in a way to prevent inadvertent disclosure of classified information.

Soldiers were especially cautioned how to screen information to family members and close friends. They were instructed not to send classified information through the mail or to refer to Army units, military installations, transportation facilities, the effect of enemy operations, code systems or current location.

"Is it safe to tell my mother where we're going?"

BITS OF CARELESS TALK
ARE PIECED TOGETHER BY THE ENEMY

England
Convoy sails for tonight

An alarming poster warns soldiers that even snakes are considered to be more safe than lips that give away troop movements, ship sailings and war equipment.

This poster warns that even the smallest amounts of information overheard by the enemy could add up to a big problem.

LESS DANGEROUS

THAN CARELESS TALK

DON'T DISCUSS TROOP MOVEMENTS · SHIP SAILINGS · WAR EQUIPMENT

Good news from home

TANKS
PLANES
GUNS
SHIPS

MORE PRODUCTION

American Industry Responds

War production solves unemployment

The need for war materials created labor opportunities that beefed up a work force that was struggling to recover following the Great Depression. Industry was created to manufacture weapons, machinery and other needed items for military action in World War II.

President Roosevelt noted that the labor efforts by civilians at home to support troops were as critical to winning the war as the efforts of the troops themselves.

Workers were reminded that often the success of an operation relied on the availability and quality of items manufactured back on the home front.

Tank production became one of the leading industries during the war. America became a forerunner in world-wide military equipment production.

Workers employed by Studebaker had reason to be proud when they saw pictures of the World War "Flying Fortress" bomber heading out to defend our country. Many aircraft and tanks performed well, thanks to the success of American craftsmen.

The proudest assignment in our 90-year history

Studebaker BUILDS WRIGHT CYCLONE ENGINES FOR THE *Flying Fortress*

American Industry Responds
Build it and move it

Maintenance of the New York Central Railroad created hundreds of jobs in the northeast. Known as the "Water Level Railroad," its mainline stretched east from the Lake Erie shoreline by way of the Erie Canal, Hudson River and into New York City.

The electrification of the Pennsylvania Railroad created an opportunity for mass transit that enabled passengers and supplies to connect with other parts of the country in large-scale travel. The railroad was the largest in scale by traffic and revenues during the war.

"There's another good reason we'll win this war !"

The ability of the American work force to mass produce bombs enabled the United States military to continue to implement intense attacks without hesitation. The large production guaranteed an overwhelming ability for military power.

Workers were instilled with the idea that the quality and amount of their production helped to send a personal message to the enemy.

The Army-Navy "E" award was presented to companies during World War II for excellence in production of war equipment. A total of 4,283 companies received the award during the war.

American Industry Responds
At home and abroad

"THROUGH HELL AND HIGH WATER"

THE JEEP FROM WILLYS-OVERLAND

Two years before the declaration of war, the U.S. Army had asked auto manufacturers to submit designs for simple and efficient military vehicles. Willys-Overland eventually won the bid. The Willys-Overland Jeep became an icon of military transport in World War II. By the war's end, over 600,000 jeeps had rolled off its assembly lines.

The Jeep calls them Daddy...

THE QUARTERMASTER CORPS OF THE U.S. ARMY AND THE CIVILIAN ENGINEERS OF WILLYS-OVERLAND

We pay public tribute here, to the Engineers of Willys—the most highly lauded automotive engineering staff that the pressure and inspiration of war have brought to light.

These are the men whose engineering skill and creative minds, added to those of the Quartermaster Corps of the U.S. Army, gave birth to the amazing Jeep of today. No other single mobile unit is so typical of modern mechanized war. And it *proves*, beyond question, that the Willys Go-Devil *Engine* and the defense-time Willys *Americar* were no "door step" babies, but legitimate offspring of fine engineering practice that is both fundamentally sound and reliable. Willys-Overland Motors, Inc., Toledo, Ohio.

TODAY do your part. Conserve rubber and other materials vital to war equipment. Buy defense stamps and bonds. Pay taxes with a smile. Whatever the total price you pay, it will be as nothing compared to the value of continued Freedom. . . . . . TOMORROW, make your first new post-war car a Willys—"The Jeep in Civvies."

Jeeps, engineered to be safe and efficient, were useful troop transport vehicles. The Willys-Overland featured four-wheel drive, an open-air cab, and a rifle rack mounted under the windshield.

INVENT for VICTORY

ALL AMERICANS WHO HAVE AN INVENTION OR AN IDEA WHICH MIGHT BE USEFUL TO THEIR COUNTRY ARE URGED TO SEND IT IMMEDIATELY TO

NATIONAL INVENTORS COUNCIL.
DEPARTMENT OF COMMERCE-WASHINGTON, D.C.

LIKE OLD MAN RIVER
they "just keep rollin' along"

General Motors, like many other auto manufacturers, adapted its factories in order to produce large quantities of military vehicles and aircraft during World War II.

The National Inventors Council was formed in 1940 under the Office of National Technical Services to provide a clearinghouse for inventions that might prove useful to the cause of national defense and to bring those inventions to the attention of the armed forces. One of the first inventions was a mercury dry cell battery with a two-month lifetime guarantee for walkie-talkie use by downed pilots.

IN ACTIVE SERVICE
for America's Two Great Armies!

In 1942, Greyhound Bus became a major carrier of troops heading to the east and west. This image shows servicemen from the Army, Navy and Marines, merging with working citizens.

In this ad, American Locomotive vowed to keep "America in motion" by providing transportation for both military and civilian passengers.

REPRINTED WITH PERMISSION OF PEERLESS MFG. CO AND ALCO PRODUCTS

With rationing of gas and tires, Americans opted to use passenger trains and buses in place of travelling by car, especially on longer excursions. Train trips became particularly popular.

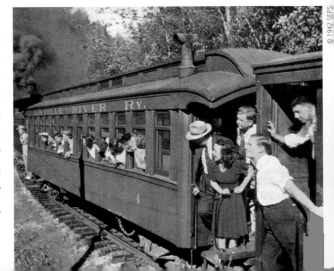

© 1942 SEPS

Transportation

America on the move

Mass transportation was vital to the movement of troops and material. With obstacles like gas rationing and a shortage of reliable cars facing them, civilians also gravitated to the mass transit system but never forgot to put the military's needs before their own.

The site of troop trains and buses became symbols of pride as soldiers moved through small communities across the country.

Pontiac advertised that their engineers had taken special consideration in developing an engine that would not infringe on any materials vital to national defense.

DEFENSE FIRST WITH OLDSMOBILE

FAMOUS BIRTHDAYS
Michael Crichton, Oct. 23
author, producer

With war on the horizon, Oldsmobile produced a movie advertisement attempting to promote sales just prior to the World War II crackdown in auto sales. In the meantime, General Motors Cadillac and Oldsmobile divisions produced the first automatic mass-produced transmission for passenger vehicles. Its use during the war greatly increased its marketing value following the war.

HYDRA-MATIC

FAMOUS BIRTHDAYS
Stephanie Powers, Nov. 2
actress
Martin Scorsese, Nov. 17
director, screenwriter and producer

Army cooks were challenged on holidays to provide feasts and other goodies for servicemen. Thanksgiving Day meals were full course treats, complete with all the trimmings.

The Metro Daily News
FINAL EDITION

NOVEMBER 28, 1942

COCONUT GROVE FIRE KILLS 492 IN BOSTON

On the George Burns and Gracie Allen radio show, sponsor Spam first introduced the "Sammy the Pig" singing commercial. Soon, young people across America were doing their own "singing pig" renditions.

General Mills was busy marketing products that would speed along the cooking process for busy war wives. This advertisement, suggesting how Bisquick could be used each day, appealed to family life and appreciation for the hardworking labor force.

'S BE KIND TO HUSBANDS WEEK!

Keep him purring! So easy...just tell him he's terrific... and feed him nobly. Let Bisquick help you. It's a short cut to so many foods with man-appeal. And it's calamity-proof!

You'll feel like a lady of leisure, when you follow those simple directions on the package — for ten basic bakings. You save almost half your work (no struggles with sifters).

Success is a sure thing because Bisquick is a blend of six quality ingredients ... blended more skilfully than is possible by hand. Tested by Betty Crocker and her staff. Reliable.

Yes, this is "Be Kind to Husbands" Week. Easy, with Bisquick! Order the *new improved* Bisquick today.

Free! Two oz. jar famous Lake Shore Honey. Guaranteed pure, uniformly delicious. Comes in attractive honeycomb jar. To get yours, mail a postcard to Betty Crocker, Dept. 1370, Minneapolis, Minnesota, by March 15, 1942.

PAMPER HIM WITH THESE!

WE MIX ALL SIX TO SAVE YOU WORK!
Pure vegetable shortening, baking powder, Gold Medal "Kitchen-tested" Flour, salt, sugar, powdered milk.

Hear Betty Crocker's cooking talks, Wed. and Fri. mornings, CBS, 10.00 o'clock Eastern Standard Time; 9:00 Central Time; 9:30 Mountain Time; 8:30 Pacific Time.

What Made Us Laugh

"Here comes the Washington plane now."

"Taxi!"

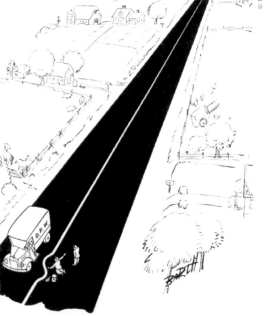

"He pushed me!"

"I told you not to peck at turtles!"

"It's all right now, Henry, I've found the bullets!"

"There's Daphne III, Bold King, Princess Sandra, Gunnymede Barker, and one of my children!"

"It's a disturbing thought, but ten years from now we may refer to this as 'The Good Old Days.'"

Advertisements for menswear of the time appealed to class and urban style. Here, *The Saturday Evening Post* recommends suits that were approved during a fashion review in New York.

Although this sailor might have looked forward to a package from home, he doesn't appreciate this hand-knitted tie from Aunt Mabel.

Love from Aunt Mabel

He-Man Jury Picks Spring Clothe

"...drab, dreary colors, won't do this spring..."

"...Manufacturers have even invented new materials..."

Early this year, came leading clothing merchants from all over the U. S. to jam a fashion show in New York. What they saw were suits, shirts, ties, hats, socks and shoes—as put together in smart color combinations by men experts of the Retail Men's Wear Council. These style selections show a cross-section of the spring lines of America's leading manufacturers ... many of them POST advertisers. *"The secret of dressing well,"* says the jury, *"is to pick a head-to-foot color plan. And stick to your plan."*

"... our jury uncovered a new kind of tweed completely without harsh fuzz ... no scratch ... no itch." This new type tweed-shetland is light in weight, smooth as a horse's nose The ever useful flannels are lighter, softer, sleeker ... cool to the touch. Many are vestless. Worsteds are feather-weight. Some inventive mind married gabardine to covert and produced another handsome fabric—India whipcord—nice to see and fee

"... How to be well-dressed this year"

These four fashion quickies are just samples. In the leading men's wear stores you can see many new styles and color combinations in shirts, suits, ties, socks, shoes, hats and other accessories—all to help you buy wisely. Look for this Post page in the windows of your favorite store ... Then go in and ask your salesman to show you the new spring style combinations picked from America's leading nationally advertised brands.

THE SATURDAY EVENING

POST

CHARLES KAISER

Men's Fashion

Dressing sharp

The Arrow shirt concept of dressing "sharp" described the mood of men's dress. Suits, ties and hats were the style for almost every occasion, from a day at work to an evening out.

Advertisements of the day reflected the image as pictures appeared in magazines showing men riding bicycles and exercising in suits and ties. Men were even depicted in full dress attire at casual restaurants or playing cards in a laid-back setting.

However, men didn't sacrifice all just to maintain a "sharp" look; most clothing manufacturers of the time stressed that their clothes were not made with materials needed for military usage.

UP-AND-COMERS

Voted "Most Likely to Succeed" in college and by gad, they *are* succeeding! As well groomed as Kentucky Derby colts. They wear Arrow White Shirts such as left, Arrow Hitt, broadcloth with non-wilt collar and Arrow Gordon, a fine oxford.

KILLER

His studied sloppiness slays nobody—except himself. A nice, easy-going guy who ought to treat himself to Arrow Shirts. Their "Mitoga" figure-fit (sloped shoulders, curved waist, tapered sleeves) do wonders for that unmade-bed look.

The Arrow shirt was first developed in New York City as "the shirt that was sharp 24/7."

MR. BIG

No Simon Legree, he—not really. Folks used to think he got red with rage—it was his tight collars. Everything's oke now that he wears Arrow Shirts whose Sanforized label means less than 1% fabric shrinkage! Get *yourself* some Arrow White Shirts now. *Cluett, Peabody & Co., Inc., Troy, N.Y.*

ARROW SHIRTS
→→→

★ BUY U. S. DEFENSE BONDS AND STAMPS ★

Jarman Shoes were considered to be one of the most fashionable of the time. These stylish "Sportables" are a good example of the two-toned coloring popular in 1942.

FAMOUS BIRTHDAYS
Donna Mills, Dec. 11 actress

Women's Fashion

Elegant but simple

Ladies' clothing in 1942 had an eloquent look, but was very simply made, often with rayon, since there was a limited supply of wool.

Most clothing of the time emphasized solid colors, with wedding attire featuring plain, ivory suits.

Most ladies attempted to make their clothing last as long as they could. That meant repairing snags, sewing on new buttons and storing clothing in an appropriate manner to last indefinitely.

The same was true with accessories, such as scarves and socks, which were often subject to sock darner repair kits and other saving measures.

Safety was another factor in clothing; garments needed to be work-efficient and adaptable to quick movement when blackout sirens sounded.

Jacket suits were a refined and popular choice for ladies' fashion, with matching accessories added to polish off the look.

Busy women wore clothing that allowed for everyday tasks, including shopping, work responsibilities or chores at home. But even a trip to the grocery store required proper attire.

Despite the need to be practical, women still found ways to put together and show off a dashing outfit.

FAMOUS BIRTHDAYS
Calvin Klein, Nov. 19 fashion designer
Joe Biden, Nov. 20 Vice President
Jimi Hendrix, Nov. 27 musician

LIFE

Boston superstar Ted Williams assisted his dependent mother with finances, and then enlisted in the Navy. Rather than accept an easy assignment, he joined the V-5 program, intent on becoming a Naval aviator. After receiving training at Amherst College and Jacksonville, Florida, he eventually served as an instructor in Pensacola.

UNITED STATES MARINE CORPS

Major League Baseball Takes Strange Turn

Major League baseball in 1942 included many unusual twists. Superstar Ted Williams not only achieved the extremely rare batting triple crown, but he also enlisted in the Navy on May 22.

For over a decade, the New York Yankees won every World Series they reached until 1942 when they lost, four games to one, to the St. Louis Cardinals. St. Louis pitcher Johnny Beazley won two games and the Yankees' Phil Rizzuto led all regulars with a .381 average.

Joe Gordon of the Yankees won the American League Most Valuable Player award; the Cardinals' Mort Cooper captured the National League title. New York Giants player Mel Ott led the National League in home runs.

In the Negro League World Series, the Kansas City Monarchs dropped the Homestead Grays, four games to none.

This humourous shot of the search for a foul ball used in an Agfa film advertisement demonstrates the wide appeal of baseball in 1942.

"I didn't see you at our ball game last Saturday, Reverend."

The Silver Screen

1942 was an important year for Australian native Errol Flynn, professionally and personally. He starred as a boxer in *Gentleman Jim* and he became naturalized as a U.S. citizen.

Film icons

Films released in 1942 strove to provide both a reflection of a world at war as well as an entertaining escape from that difficult world.

Set in occupied Morocco during World War II, *Casablanca* was both timely and inspirational with its story line centered around personal sacrifice for the greater good. Although it was not a top money-maker in 1942, the movie has since become as iconic as its two stars, Humphrey Bogart and Ingrid Bergman.

1942 brought the release of another film centered in World War II, William Wyler's *Mrs. Miniver.* In the film, which went on to receive 6 Academy Awards, Greer Garson stars as a mother and wife trying to protect her family in war-torn England.

Not all films that came out that year touched on the war. Disney released its fifth movie, *Bambi.* Westerns, like Hopalong Cassidy's *Undercover Man* and Gene Autry's *Bells of Capistrano*, were popular. And, of course, Bob Hope and Bing Crosby continued their successful pairing with the comedy *Road to Morocco.*

Tops at the Box Office

Mrs. Miniver
Reap the Wild Wind
Random Harvest
Yankee Doodle Dandy
Road to Morocco
Holiday Inn
Bambi

Honorable Mention

Casablanca
Pride of the Yankees
Woman of the Year

Bing Crosby was a success several times over in 1942. "White Christmas," one of his most well-known songs, became a hit after he performed it in the movie *Holiday Inn.*

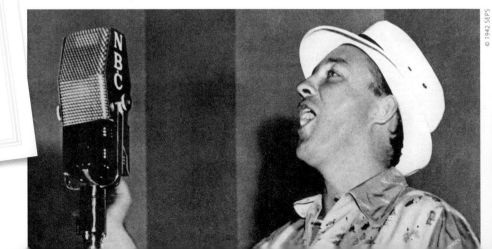

In the film *Holiday Inn*, Fred Astaire, dancing here with co-star Marjorie Reynolds, joined in a friendly entertainment competition with Bing Crosby.

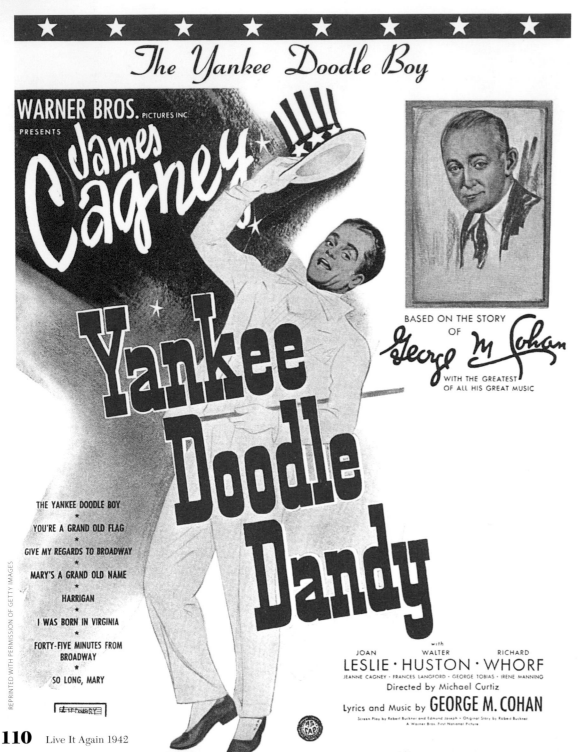

The movie *Yankee Doodle Dandy* was a biographical musical film based on the life of actor, singer, dancer, producer and playwright George M. Cohan. The part of Cohan, once described as "the man who owns Broadway," was played by James Cagney. The movie featured such patriotic tunes as "The Yankee Doodle Boy," Cohan's trademark piece which was drawn from the Revolutionary War.

The 1942 film *The Pride of the Yankees* documents the life of baseball great Lou Gehrig from his historical run of 1,230 consecutive games to the drama of battling a dreaded illness, ALS, which has since been referred to as Lou Gehrig's disease. Among those playing in the movie were some of Gehrig's (played by Gary Cooper) real-life teammates such as Bill Dickey and Babe Ruth. The movie has been lauded for its appeal to the female audience of 1942 through the delicate intertwining of Gehrig's relationship with his wife, Eleanor.

1942's *Woman of the Year* was the first of nine movies to star off-screen lovers Spencer Tracy and Katherine Hepburn. The movie intertwined the lives of Sam Craig and feminist Tess Harding (Tracy and Hepburn) who compete with each other and fall in love while working as journalists for the same New York newspaper. The movie won an Academy Award and Hepburn was nominated for Best Actress in a Leading Role.

SAMUEL GOLDWYN
Presents
GARY COOPER
THE PRIDE OF THE YANKEES

Teresa WITH Walter
WRIGHT · BRENNAN
and
BABE RUTH
himself

VELOZ AND YOLANDA
RAY NOBLE AND ORCHESTRA

It's the Great American Story!

Directed by
SAM WOOD

SCREEN PLAY BY JO SWERLING & HERMAN J. MANKIEWICZ
ORIGINAL STORY BY PAUL GALLICO

Glenn Miller led the way in the rise of the popularity of swing music during the war years. Miller, an American jazz musician, arranger, composer, and band leader, introduced such popular tunes as "Chattanooga Choo Choo" and "Little Brown Jug." In December of 1944, his plane went missing over the English Channel and was never recovered.

Benny Goodman quickly took the title of "King of Swing." His early jazz and swing style emerged into a new kind of swing that was not only made popular by his orchestration, but also by several movie appearances. Goodman's style served as a transition to rock, pop and jazz music in the early 1950s.

Jimmy Dorsey, often referred to as "JD," was a popular jazz clarinetist, saxophonist, trumpeter, composer and big band leader. In the 1930s and 40s, he had 11 number one hits. One of his most noted traits was his enhancement of other popular musicians, such as Bing Crosby, who recorded his famous hit "Pennies from Heaven" with the backing of the Jimmy Dorsey orchestra.

JOE VENUTI

Jimmy Dorsey

Glenn Miller

Benny Goodman

EDDY DUCHIN

BOBBY HAGGART

JACK TEAGARDEN

GENE KRUPA

HARRY JAMES

TEX BENECKE

TOMMY DORSE

America Tunes in to the "Swing Era"

Beginning in the 1930s, the likes of Benny Goodman, Glenn Miller, Jimmy and Tommy Dorsey and Artie Shaw introduced a swing style of music that was initially seen as somewhat wild and controversial. However, as the big band sound continued to gain momentum, it soon became associated with lifting the spirits of a nation at war.

The music world supported the war effort in several ways. Musicians recorded V-discs, a series of records which were made, by arrangement of the U.S. government, for enlisted men overseas.

Artists such as Miller and Shaw joined up with the military in order to help bolster music among the armed forces. While Miller was traveling with his wartime band in Europe, Shaw founded a band which served a similar purpose in the Pacific Theater.

© 1942 SEPS

JACK JENNY

ALVINO REY

ARLIE
RNET

The Metro Daily News
FINAL EDITION

THE WEATHER
City and Intra-State
Snow, Colder

VOLUME 67 — No. 181

CHARLESTON, WEST VIRGINIA

29 PAGES   FIVE CENTS

AUGUST 1, 1942

UNION MUSICIAN RECORDINGS BARRED

James Petrillo, leader of American Federation of Musicians, orders bar on union musicians recording new music other than v-discs intended for servicemen.

Top Hits of 1942

White Christmas Bing Crosby

He Wears a Pair of Silver Wings Kay Kyser

Tangerine Jimmy Dorsey

Moonlight Cocktail Glenn Miller

Blues In The Night Woody Herman

(I've Got a Gal In) Kalamazoo Glenn Miller

Jersey Bounce Benny Goodman

Sleepy Lagoon Harry James

Jingle, Jangle, Jingle Kay Kyser

Somebody Else Is Taking My Place Benny Goodman

Deep in the Heart of Texas Alvino Rey

Paper Doll Mills Brothers

Don't Sit Under the Apple Tree (With Anyone Else but Me) Glenn Miller

I Don't Want to Walk Without You Harry James

Rose O'Day (The Filla-Da-Gusha Song) Freddy Martin

People Are Funny

Radio show made debut

The famed comedy talk show *People are Funny* made its debut on April 3, 1942 with Art Baker as the host. A year later, Baker was replaced by Art Linkletter, who made the show so popular that it spilled over into the literary world as well.

Other popular radio broadcasts of the time included *The Jack Benny Program, Fred Allen Show, Your Hit Parade, Lux Radio Theater, The Longer Ranger, The Green Hornet, The Shadow* and *Suspense*.

Ongoing series included, *Amos 'n Andy, Captain Midnight, Fibber McGee and Molly, Sherlock Holmes* and *Whistler*.

In addition to music, variety, comedy, mystery and drama, many of the shows included various forms of patriotism to reflect the mood of the country during the ongoing war.

Actor Walter Pidgeon, co-star of the popular and acclaimed film *Mrs. Miniver*, was caught on camera during a broadcast reporting information about the War Production Board's progress.

"Will Bill be reclassified? What happens to Dick, now that he's given up the gas station? When will Mary find her ration book? Does Uncle Joe win his battle with the priorities board? Tune in tomorrow at this time and ——"

John Flynn and Virginia Moore are pictured rehearsing for the radio show *You Can't Do Business With Hitler*. The program was written and produced by the Office of War Information.

The popular comic team of Abbott and Costello launched their own weekly radio show on October 8, 1942. They became one of the most popular and highest paid entertainer teams in the world. They made 36 films together between 1940 and 1956. In 1942, they were the top box office draw with a reported income of $10 million.

English actor Cedric Hardwicke reads his lines for the War Production Board's Blue Network radio show *Three Thirds of the Nation*. The program was a popular information program during the war years.

Merry Christmas TO PUPPY FROM THE FAMILY

PUPPY SOAP

FLEA POWDER

CHARLES KAISER

"... an' while I keep him covered, you grab the sack, run like mad for the bathroom an' lock yourself in. Then I'll chase him back up the chimney."

"First, I want some explanation on last year!"

"I'm gonna try again. My mother wasn't listening."

More *The Saturday Evening Post Covers*

The Saturday Evening Post covers were works of art, many illustrated by famous artists of the time, including Norman Rockwell. Most of the 1942 covers have been incorporated within the previous pages of this book; the few that were not are presented on the following pages for your enjoyment.

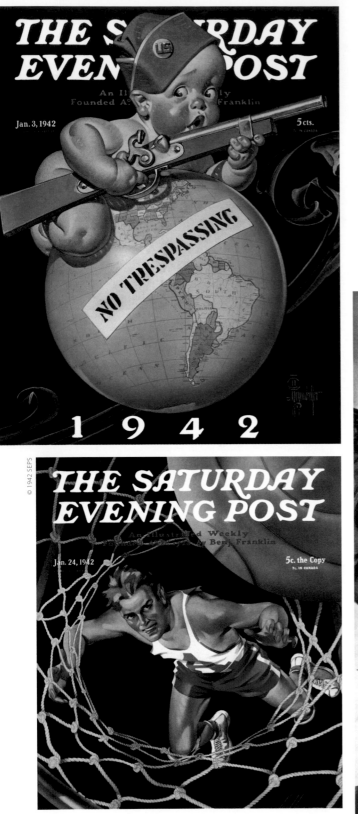

JAPAN'S ISLANDS
OF MYSTERY
By WILLARD PRICE

MORE FAMOUS BIRTHDAYS

January 1
Country Joe McDonald, American musician

January 2
Dennis Hastert, American politician and former Speaker of the United States House of Representatives
Hugh Shelton, American Chairman of the Joint Chiefs of Staff

January 8
Yvette Mimieux, American actress

January 17
Nancy Parsons, American actress

January 19
Michael Crawford

January 25
Carl Eller, American football player

February 2
Graham Nash, American (English-born) rock musician (CSNY)

February 5
Roger Staubach, American football player

February 13
Peter Tork, American musician and actor

February 15
Sherry Jackson, American actress

February 19
Paul Krause, American football player

February 20
Phil Esposito, Canadian hockey player
Mitch McConnell, American politician

February 25
Karen Grassle, American actress

February 28
Brian Jones, English musician (The Rolling Stones)

March 2
John Irving, American author
Lou Reed, American singer-songwriter and guitarist

March 4
Gloria Gaither, American gospel songwriter

March 7
Tammy Faye Bakker, American evangelist, singer and television personality

March 9
John Cale, Welsh composer and musician (The Velvet Underground)

March 12
Jimmy Wynn, American baseball player

March 13
Dave Cutler, American software engineer
Scatman John, American musician

March 26
Erica Jong, American author

March 27
Michael York, English actor

March 28
Jerry Sloan, American basketball coach

March 29
Scott Wilson, American actor

April 2
Leon Russell, American singer, songwriter, pianist, and guitarist

April 3
Marsha Mason, American actress
Wayne Newton, American singer

April 6
Barry Levinson, American film producer and director

April 15
Kenneth Lay, American businessman
Julie Sommars, American actress

April 23
Sandra Dee, American actress

April 24
Barbra Streisand, American singer, theatre and film actress, composer

April 26
Bobby Rydell, American singer

May 5
Tammy Wynette, American country singer

May 12
Ian Dury, British musician

May 17
Taj Mahal, American singer and guitarist

May 20
David Proval, American actor

May 22
Calvin Simon, American musician (P Funk)

May 26
Levon Helm, American musician (The Band)

May 28
Stanley B. Prusiner, American scientist, recipient of the Nobel Prize in Physiology of Medicine.

June 3
Frank McRae, American actor

June 17
Roger Steffens, Reggae archivist, actor, author, Bob Marley biographer

June 24
Michele Lee, American actress, singer and dancer

June 27
Bruce Johnston, American musician
(The Beach Boys)

July 2
Vincente Fox, President of Mexico

July 4
Floyd Little, American football player

July 8
Janice Pennington, American model

July 9
Richard Roundtree, American actor

July 13
Roger McGuinn, American musician (The
Byrds)

July 24
Chris Sarandon, American actor

July 29
Tony Sirico, American actor

August 19
Fred Dalton Thompson, American
politician and actor

August 20
Isaac Hayes, American singer and actor

August 27
"Captain" Daryl Dragon, American
musician (The Captain and Tennille)

August 28
Sterling Morrison, American musician

August 31
Isao Aoki, Japanese golfer

September 19
Freda Payne, American singer and actress

September 22
David Stern, American commissioner of the
National Basketball Association

September 28
Marshall Bell, American actor

September 29
Madeline Kahn, American actress

September 30
Frankie Lymon, American singer

October 6
Britt Ekland, Swedish actress
Fred Travalena, American comedian and
impressionist

October 12
Melvin Franklin, American musician (The
Temptations)

October 13
Jerry Jones, American football team owner

October 19
Andrew Vachss, American author and
attorney

October 20
Earl Hindman, American actor

October 21
Elvin Bishop, American musician

October 22
Annette Funicello, American actress

October 29
Bob Ross, American painter and television
presenter

October 31
David Ogden Stiers, American actor and
voice-over artist

November 1
Larry Flynt, American publisher
Marcia Wallace, American actress and
comedienne

November 18
Linda Evans, American actress
Susan Sullivan, American actress

November 27
Henry Carr, American athlete
Manolo Blahnik, Spanish shoe designer

November 28
Paul Warfield, American football player

December 4
Gemma Jones, British actress

December 9
Dick Butkus, American football player

December 11
Donna Mills, American actress

December 12
Peter Sarstedt, British musician

December 17
Paul Butterfield, American musician

December 20
Bob Hayes, American athlete

December 21
Carla Thomas, American singer

December 23
Jorma Kaukonen, American musician
(Jefferson Airplane, Hot Tuna)

December 27
Charmian Carr, American actress

December 30
Betty Aberlin, American actress
Allan Gotthelf, American philosopher

December 31
Andy Summers, English guitarist

Facts and Figures of 1942

President of the U.S.
Franklin Delano Roosevelt
Vice President of the U.S.
Henry A. Wallace

Population of the U. S.
134,860,000
Births
2,989,000

High School Graduates
Males: 577,000
Females: 666,000

Average Salary for full time employee:
$1,729.00
Minimum Wage (per hour): $0.30

Average cost for:

Bread (lb.) 09

Bacon (lb.) 39

Butter (lb) 47

Eggs (Doz.)....................................48

Milk (gal.)......................................60

Potatoes (10 lbs.)........................34

Coffee (lb.) 28

Sugar (5 lbs.) 34

Gasoline (gal.).............................19

Movie Ticket................................27

Postage Stamp............................03

Car......................................$890.00

Single-family home $3700.00

Notable Events

Enrico Fermi's team builds world's first nuclear reactor.

Harvard University invents Napalm.

Johnson & Johnson invents Duct Tape which was originally created for use in the military, was army green and was referred to as "Duck" tape because it is waterproof.

Pauli Ström invents disposable diapers.

John Atanasoff and Clifford Berry create the ABC Computer, the first electronic digital computer.

The lumbar epidural is introduced in obstetrics.

The weekly magazine *Yank* is first published. The magazine, which was written by and published for enlisted men, ends publication in 1945.

Kelloggs introduces the cereal Raisin Bran.

Dannon, the first American yogurt company, is established.

Construction begins on the Alaska Highway. The highway opens to military traffic by November 20, but is not open to public traffic until 1948.

Sports Winners
(Several championships not played because of WWII)

NFL: Washington Redskins defeat Chicago Bears
World Series: St. Louis Cardinals defeat New York Yankees
Stanley Cup: Toronto Maple Leafs defeat Detroit Red Wings
The Masters: Byron Nelson wins
PGA Championship: Sam Snead wins

Live It Again 1942

PROJECT EDITOR	Richard Stenhouse
ASSISTANT EDITOR	Erika Mann
ART DIRECTOR	Brad Snow
COPYWRITER	Jim Langham
MANAGING EDITOR	Barb Sprunger
PRODUCTION ARTIST	Edith Teegarden
COPY EDITOR	Amanda Ladig
PHOTOGRAPHY SUPERVISOR	Tammy Christian
NOSTALGIA EDITOR	Ken Tate
COPY SUPERVISOR	Michelle Beck
GRAPHIC ARTS SUPERVISOR	Ronda Bechinski
EDITORIAL DIRECTOR	Jeanne Stauffer
PUBLISHING SERVICES DIRECTOR	Brenda Gallmeyer

Printed in China
First Printing: 2010
Library of Congress Number: 2009904214
ISBN: 978-1-59635-273-5

Customer Service
LiveItAgain.com
(800) 829-5865

1 2 3 4 5 6 7 8 9